BRIDGES TO
RIVERS TO CROSS
MOUNTAINS TO MOVE

early writings...

BRIDGES TO BUILD
RIVERS TO CROSS
MOUNTAINS TO MOVE

poems on love, struggle and motivation

KAYO
KRAAL Y. CHARLES

Introduction by Patricia Flowers

Edited by Belinda A. Crichlow

PAGACommunications, Inc.
NEW YORK

This book is a work of fiction. Names, characters, places and incidents are either the product of the author's imagination or are used fictitiously. Any resemblance to actual events or locales or persons, living or dead, is entirely coincidental

Permissions Department
PAGACommunications, Inc.
6 Woodland Road
Valley Stream, NY 11581.
(516) 792-9538
PAGACom@aol.com

ISBN: 0-9701768-0-5

To the memory of
Bro. Mike
My partner for life and beyond

Acknowledgments

*I would like to thank my mother and father for making me the man I
am and will become, teaching me to never settle
To my sister Phentresse for inspiring me through music
To Patricia for inspiring me by action
To Belinda for being a part of my life
To Kirk... who believes
And to my extended poetic family who inspire me every single day
"Continue to move obstacles that are in your path"*

Introduction

It all happened at The Nuyorican Poet's Café, which is well known for its abilities to provide a ready spotlight to street-known, up-and-comers and gusty closet-artists. On that night in particular, Kraal was that gusty closet-artist. Four of us were vibing at the bar, taking in the stifling cigarette smoke and poetry -- two things synonymous with Nuyorican Poet's Café. Our two friends were known poets who orbited that circle. They had no reservations with taking the stage. Kraal and I did. We were mere spectators on foreign poetry grounds. What began as a playful gesture, mushroomed into a dare, then an all out hijacking. Our names were placed on the open-mic list. I took to the stage half high from the adrenaline rush, my knees softened, my voice swayed and I blanked. I was only able to get out a modicum of a poem I'd committed to memory. Writing poetry was one thing but performing was another animal. The audience encouraged me to go on, but I could not. I left the stage feeling relieved, not embarrassed, because the energy at Nuyorican makes it almost impossible for that to happen. "I'm so nervous," Kraal whispered. He was also wary of unleashing his poetry in a room full of white people. Not because it was blasphemous, but because it was empowering to black ears. In America, words that are empowering to black ears are considered blasphemous, dangerous and untrue. But, I've heard this particular poem once before when he performed it at Medgar Evers College, where he was attending at the time. He received a standing ovation, which was rightfully deserved. That ovation was given to him by a roomful of black people. The crowd at Nuyorican that night, and any particular night is fairly mixed but mostly white. It wasn't cowardly of him to be nervous. He realized the truth and the power of his poem. Thus, acknowledging the power of words and the activity which it sparks. This particular poem is a thorough history lesson, a testimony of endurance and a wake up call to strengthen us. But, sometimes our truth is so ugly it sounds like curse words, and so beautiful, we try to conceal them. That poem took six long months to write. He began writing it while completing his internship at one of the top advertising companies in Austria. He researched long and hard. He made sure his metaphors had meaning and were not only cute sounding. Although he was nervous, we both knew he was truly ready to perform. He stepped on stage and performed what is now considered his signature poem, MOUNTAINS. He gave everyone an "eargasm" that night. Like a baby cub possessing the thundering roar of his father, he surprised the hell out of everyone. He roared and they roared back in appreciation. That night changed his life. He saw for the first time, a gallery where his hidden drawings can finally be displayed. He found that artistic part of himself and it was simultaneously acknowledged. Most people spend their entire life in pursuit of what he experienced that very moment. If that moment were a metal, it would have been platinum. It was that precious and untarnished.

He went on to perform (less nervously) at many other well known venues and far away places, like, the very first Poetry Expo in Portugal, The Historical Black College & University Exposition, The Dr. Betty Shabazz Memorial and The Paul Robeson Bicentennial Celebration, to name a few. Upon his many returns to the Nuyorican Poets Café's stage, in the summer of 1998, he stepped off a Nuyorican's Poetry Grand Slam youngest winner. But more importantly, he's continued to study and write poetry.

Kraal is a fiend of the spoken and written word. He is easily inspired. His ability to draw inspiration from a lifeless plant sometimes befuddles me. While most 16-year-old boys sought the latest fashion trend, hottest rap song and cutest girl, Kraal was huddled in my bedroom sharing his plans of becoming an entrepreneur. There's something beautiful and rare about that kind of drive and determination. With all fairness, Kraal has a strong weakness for women and a stronger talent for making them weaker for him. To his credit, his attraction has never caused him to vacillate from his goals. As I look back at what possibly could have ignited the fire in him, I can attribute it to one single fact. Although he came from a loving family, there wasn't a scintilla of evidence provided by his environment in East Flatbush, Brooklyn that assured him, he would grow up to be an artist. But his determination was so strong that he surpassed all expectancies his environment might have defined for him. In the end, it didn't take a reputable family name or a trust fund to make things happen, just strong will, and Kraal has it in abundance.

Hearing Kraal's cave-deep baritone voice in person while he performs is one experience. But, reading his poetry and witnessing how intricately his words are molded together, will surely take you into a whole other dimension of his work. I am very proud that he's gathered together these selected pieces along with the accompanied CD, which features the actual 1998 Nuyorican Poetry Slam performance. This book is truly a complete experience for your senses.

Patricia Flowers

Love...

Wrestling The Word

Rap does not cause violence
Because
Poetry does
Haven't you heard, it maybe absurd
I woke up this morning wrestling the word
She gave me elbows of passionate prose
I arose to my toes and fell in her clothes' line
By design she left me in shock
I swung in defense and she threw up a writer's block
With word capacity she showed her tenacity
With such velocity, she swung her verbosity
I duck and dodged, I bobbed and weaved
But I tell you it was no use
She caused friction with her diction
It must have been verbal abuse
So I went along for the ride
I had to run and hide
For the words she threw at me
Just kept hitting me in the side
And if it was one word, I could understand
But they kept coming at me in chorus
And some of these words were unknown to man
Somebody quick hand me a thesaurus
And don't tell me poetry does not cause violence
Because I will go insane
Because here I am, I'm wrestling the word

And I think the word is pain
And don't sing me anymore nursery rhymes
Because I will go berserk
Sticks and stones may break your bones
But I tell you words hurt
Because she gave it to me raw
This pain I can't endure
And that's why I don't want to make love to that
That, that poet anymore

No Love No Poet

I don't want to make love to that poet anymore
You see, maybe you could understand my plight
Every argument, every fight
Was a poem that she would write
And when she spoke about sex
Damn! That got me vexed
I had little breath left for the topic she had next
She made things so complex
I am better off being her friend
But every time I shied away
I felt the affliction of her pen
No challenge has been given
Yet her gauntlet has risen
I must shout, I want out
Trapped in this lyrical prison
Oh I don't want to make love to that poet anymore
This type of relationship I cannot treasure
You don't understand the pressure
Oh such passionate displeasure
Through her poems I perused
And realized I was not amused
I told her to stop this at once
And perversely she refused
This was the road that I chose
No way could I win
To all the men she accused
Where did this hatred begin?

I remember the days
When she would really get me hyped
She would hop up on the stage with rage
And rock an open mic
Then there was that time
That time when she tore some guy in half
She called him a low down dirty uh!
And it really made me laugh
But then my third eye started to focus
Now clearly I can see
She called him a six-foot dark-skinned muthafu..
Time out--she is talking about me!
I cried, "Censorship!" "Censorship!"
Somebody please stop her
She is ruining my life
And they watch it like a soap opera
I don't want to make love to that poet anymore
Those words that she has begotten
Has placed me rotten to the core
This side of her I never saw
I never heard those words before
And the crowd
The crowd is crying "More!" "More!" "More!"
Soooo
I had to break up with her

I Had To Break Up With Her

I had to break up with her
What more can be said?
We campaigned on mind games
That left me with aches in my head
The name of my future wife
Was stress, struggle and strife
We etched in stones, tones
That would eventually ruin my life
Sooo…
I had to break up with her.
It's not like she didn't have a clue
We faded away like an idle day
With absolutely nothing to do
Our thoughts were no longer in line
Her heart no longer etched my design
Her sentences became shorter
And she could no longer finished mine
I mean, I guess, I suppose in a way my mind froze
Written in poetry or prose
That is the way the story goes
Where in all of love did we muster such desire?
The woman I labeled a fraud and she called me a liar
Where in all eternity did our souls meet?
I say calmly, there is no harmony
Written on our musical sheet
Sooo…
I had to break up with her

She didn't cry
She didn't fret
She moved away from me in an instant
As if to say, no sweat
What was I supposed to say?
These actions found, I couldn't figure
Until the next day
I saw her with some muscle bound nnnn-brother
Right from that moment
All of our arguments seemed petty
I wanted her mind, her soul, her...
Damn I missed her already
No more time can be killed
To have her is my will
Now she is history
And the mystery is why I love her still
Sooo...
I had to make up with her
That's the way that it had to be
Another man holding her hand
When she belongs to me

What A Man Wants To Say To A Woman But Can't Find The Words

The thought of her presence
Promotes the scent of her essence
As I wonder where thou art
Those almond shaped eyes that captured my heart
How dare you be the way you are?
Leaving healthy men like me wishing upon a star
How dark is my exterior and my heart remains cold
But you are the light that shines warmly
Within the depths of my soul
How dare you beauty be more than skin deep
The mere mention of your name
Caresses me in my sleep
Lord I day dream of her arrival
To receive a tender kiss, I pray upon my bible
For you I shall live and die by the sword
The taste of your flesh be my sweet reward
Love pulsates through me like aches and pains
Like blood your soul runs through my veins
Who told you to be so attractive?
One glimpse of your face
Makes a man hyperactive
Judge me by my actions and not by my youth
And I will stay faithful to my attraction
In honesty and in truth
If thinking of you were a battle
I would fight for every thought
Then bring you the heads

Of the men that I have fought
Just say you love me
And that is all that needs to be said
And I will bow on one knee
With this ring I thee wed

Disgusted Love Is...

... that bulging pain manifesting itself within the depths of your soul it makes you want to scream and cry and ask for mercy and ask for her back but you know that is not the role of a man so you keep the hurt within you and you dare not show it to no one especially her whose face you have to see every day of your undergraduate life you wish her to disappear for the mere sight of her makes your stomach turn and turn and turn and you don't know what to do for you want to scream and cry and ask for mercy and ask for her ...back but you know you can't do that for she made that pain that makes you heart beat irregular sometimes you want revenge sometimes you just want to know why sometimes you just want to slap the frustration out of her you want to scream and cry and ask for her ...back but your mouth would never find the words for you dare not utter them even when you're alone but you still want to know Why? Why? Why? Why? Why? Why? it just doesn't make sense it will never make sense not to me not to her not to anybody or any living soul and that is the most messed up thing about it.

Try Again

I am
A fool of love
For I move blindly
In my steps
Only to find sorrow
But like others
I do not learn from
This
But to keep
Moving
On

Humbling In Her Presence

If your beauty be the sun then let me be the night
So I could watch you rise as I wither out of sight
If your beauty be in song then let me be in tune
Let my eyes be mesmerized
Be there no rising of the moon
How can your beauty have only just begun?
As I look over the horizon
Never to see the setting sun
Isn't it ironic the way the sun shines so bright?
Yet in the midst of darkness never to see the light
Let your sun shine on my darkness
So I could see your pearly whites
And I will patent your smile
And you can hold the copyrights
Oh the love that you deliver
Gives me a shiver down my spine
Your scent has got me dizzy
Tipsy, like brandy and wine
How exalting is your presence
Could you be so sublime?
It's like I made love for the very first time
With you... you
You give me moans and groans
And I deep and dark tones
Your sensations have more communication
Then cellular phones
Let your beauty be in math

So I could tally up the total
I read books of your charms
Oh can Barnes be so Noble
I heard of you in screenplays and sonnets
But they were so hyperbolic
Yet with a devilish grin, within you I will frolic
Common English called you pretty
And slang called you "da bomb"
Computers labeled you www.whatawonderfulwomen.com
And if they refuse to sing your song
Then by God I will make them hum it
I will take your arms and heartbeat rate
And conduct them while they drum it
We will form poetry forums and summits
On your beautiful stomach
And your scent meant a great investment
While the Dow Jones plummet
Oh in this world of love and hate
Let your beauty be my fate
And I will search from state to state
Measuring in height and in weight
But the U. S can't possess you so I have to go global
I cried for you in Kosovo
And in Switzerland I yodeled
You be the cure to my roar
Tell them forget the veterinarian
I thought you were hungry so I searched Turkey
But forgot you were a vegetarian
And even in Great Britain I saw a sight rarely seen
British men held up their teacups in your name

And screamed "To the queen!" "To the queen!"
Where is the queen our master?
I looked along the edges of Mozambique
And swam to Madagascar
There they said you soaked your dreads
In the heavenly waters of Shiloh
But seek knowledge at the most prestigious college located
somewhere in Cairo
But it was there in Ethiopia
I saw the core of your essence
You see the lion within me roars...
But I humble in your presence

From The Moment...

From the moment that I saw you I wanted you
Maybe it was meant to be
Maybe it was you or just me
All I know is that in my eyes I see you
In movies or in parks or in the shadows of the dark
You shine sharp like a spark and my heart froze
Yes my passions arose and that scent
Yes that scent from my nose was you
It smelled like the mysteries of the fossils
Hundreds of heavenly gospels
So I flared up my nostrils
And I inhaled you again
I inhaled the Titanic that sailed the Atlantic
I ran frantic for roses that made me romantic
For you...oh for you I will take millions of showers
And wait billions of hours
If I could just use my powers
To make you walk only on flowers
I will
I will, but still for satisfaction
If I could just have a fraction of that pulse
That pumps volts to keep my heart in action
I am at war with your attraction
And the booming of the tank
Is leaving me outranked
I must thank God
For those moments inside my memory banks

Moments of you and I will never die
For that is my way
My inner eye flips and my heart skips
I pray for your lips
And a lunar eclipse
To still claim you as my summer's day
No addition or dissection could aid to your perfection
I will be that protection that you'll never lose
No neglecting we stood upon clouds and as we joined
We flipped a coin to see
Which mountains we could move
Next, I got vexed at the messenger of love's arrow
For he kept aiming at sparrows
I said Cupid, don't be stupid
Make your target narrow
And then we made amends from even and odd ends
And our friends told us when
She would have me whipped
I took that script and I read to the earth
For what is worth, she gave birth
And our first child was named Egypt
And all of Spain and France danced
To the heartbeat of her womb
And soon Asia would praise her I assume
And her beauty ran wild
And all of Europe watched her smile
As we laid eyes on such a surprise
Which was Ethiopia's child
And I looked at you (Ethiopia)
And I looked at her (Egypt)

Then you again for I realized from where she came
This pain that you have doctored
This beauty that you have proctored
Is the same joy that I will claim
No longer will I know or feel tomorrow's sorrows
But tell me is this real?
Is this really what I feel?
Or is this piece of reality borrowed?
Well I won't give it back, I won't!
To fight it yes I must
For I refused to be ship wrecked
And watch iron turn to rust
No power of attorney can award me of such journey
No kings with diamond rings
Can produce such priceless things
No December stranger in a manger
No baby wrapped up in a towel
No adjective or verb can describe
No pronunciation by consonant on vowel
Just you!
Just me!
Just her!
Just us!
Cause from the moment that I saw you
I wanted you.

Not A friend

How could I stay in the same room?
She has turned my brightest morning
Into something else
She was my love, yes my love of the past
How can love be lost so fast?
Sometimes I wonder
Why did she act the way she did?
And I so loathed the woman
Who should've had my kid
I was a fool to give her my love and trust
Now the mere sight of her face
Fills my heart with disgust
I have no more love, for there is no respect
Although the curves of her body still makes me erect
But I must keep my pride
And the lust I will hide
The soul, the mind and God is on my side
Now I pray for this something else to end
For I dare not speak to her
Not even as a friend

I Fail To Forget

I fail to forget the woman I loved
The body I hugged
The clitoris I rubbed
I fail to forget the bosom I cupped
The nipples I sucked
The vagina I ffff-
I fail to forget that smile on her face
The navel that I taste
The pride of my race
I fail to forget the times that we had
Good times I might add
Never can I stay mad
I fail to forget the bad taste as I rest
The frustration and stress
On the day she confessed
As long as loving eyes cannot see
And pure anger cannot stand
I will never forget the day
She told me...
She was with another man!

Watery Eyes

Water eyes have become my custom
For when it comes to women, I have no wisdom
I move blindly step after step I prance
Just a mere simulation of a fool doing a fool's dance
A fool fit for a king or a somewhat court jester
I spent my foolish career
Always trying to impress her
She who makes my heart beat faster than the norm
In the summertime I am cool
And in the winter I am warm
She who captivates life before me
Every moment with her
Develops a different plot to my story
She who has been in my dreams
Ever since I was young
Damping my bed with her sweat
Hearing her name exercising her tongue
Tall and brown-skinned she smiles at me so bright
Can you tell me if you've seen her?
For she hasn't been in my sight
I have had all forms of heights and weights
Odd shapes and sizes
Fake hair, fake nails and eye contacts
Were some of their disguises
But I've got to find her
I have searched every day of the week
I've asked the cannons and the rivers

But even they wouldn't speak
Her ways are pure majestic
Her beauty is the definition itself
Her complexion be of bronze
Eyes not of material wealth
I have walked two thousand paces
I have been to two thousand different places
I have stomped through swamps
And sanded through deserts
Just to find my sweet oasis
I have got to find her; it doesn't have to be today
I can move mountains if it gets in my way
I will give any man the fist, who ever got her pissed
I will dive the deepest abyss
For that tender sweet kiss
Can you tell me if you've seen her?
I can't give you a better description
Just know if her beauty be in a magazine
Then I must have a subscription
Intellectual in mind
Eyes focused not on stardom
There is a rose that is mine
Can it be in Spanish Harlem?
Shakespeare's summer's day cannot compare
I will search all of Uganda or even Zaire
How dare thy beauty treat me as such a wretch?
To think that I could hold you in my arms
Be so farfetched
But I got to have you, for I searched for you so much
I want a scent of satisfaction

From a taste or a touch
Or a glance
Cause one look
Can give me the power from within
But without you in my arms it's like wrestling with the
wind.

Insaaanity/Saaanity

Written by Tantra and Kayo

Tantra:

Why didn't you tell me who you really were?
From the moment we first met
I was inside and in between
The flip side/your side was the right side
I was so in love with you

From the moment we first met
I knew I wanted to be with you
And I thought you wanted to be too/so I fell in
Like a waterfall/rushing loose/flowing free/on the
Strength of who you said you could be/you taught me
How to kiss away memories of past wanna-be lovers
You were my first

It was spring and in the fall we fell in love
We even envisioned our unborn babies
Making love by candlelight/night lighting the way
Like someone from a dream
I was your queen/you were my king
My one and only/God's most precious gift to me
And I presented myself to you
Doesn't that have any meaning?

Kayo:

Many moons have gone by
Since the last time we've met

Spoons of cries I analyze
Chastise my eyes with regret
You are my queen of the palace
My weekend in Paris
I've done you wrong for so long
And still you hold no malice
You are my saaanity
And I traded you away for no more than two coins
Because the urge in my loins
Laid where all misery joins
The vision wasn't clear to me
So blurry was longevity
I fondled with emotions
And I fought my own integrity
Yes I questioned my fidelity
But her words were smooth in motion
I saw those hips and the parting of her lips
Told me nothing about devotion
I searched for explanations
And found not one that would fit
Butterflies held summits in my stomach
Working down to my pit
I told her I loved her, but I know she feels deceived
What words can I utter to make you to believe?
You are my saaanity
My inner eye, my deeper light
My clear blue sky, my natural high
The reason why I sleep at night
How could I say it in one sentence?
To forgive my past tenses

I lost all my senses
And now I face the consequences

Tantra:

Why didn't you tell me who you really were?
This is insaaane/why didn't you tell me about her?
Were you so much man?
That only two could make you feel like one?
This is the downside of love/the flip side of reality
Baby, this is insaaanity!
You are the shift in this relationship
It wasn't her
It was you who couldn't prove your manhood
To me truthfully/instead you were out there living your life
unfaithfully
I do/I do /I do /I do
Know that I am still in love with you
And the insaaanity is that I thought you vowed to always
love me too

I've got to go
But/was it alright?
Did you hold her tight?
Did you spread her legs baby?
Did you let her come inside your...

I've got to go
But/did you kiss her from head to toe?
Did you cradle her in mounds of rose petals?
So that her scent could rise?

Did you make love to her head?
Baby, did you make love to her in our bed?
Did you do her like you used to do me baby?
This is insaaanity!

We used to be like spring/in winter
Falling into place
Me falling into you/you falling into me
But I can't catch you this time
This is the downside of love
The flip side of reality
Baby, this is insaaanity!

And not even the strength of my love could hold you
And now my arms can't reach you any longer

<u>Kayo:</u>
My love I never planned it
I didn't mean to be so candid
I feel I should die, I cry to be reprimanded
I try to run from the pain
But couldn't hide from my guilt
I covered myself in shame
But found no comfort in my quilt
How weakened is your tolerance
Now your patience walks on stilts
Your heart can no longer race or flip
Off this relationship that we've built
I have broken our sacred creed
Avariciously I found the need

Now what words can I say to you?
To erase this evil deed

You now exist in the corners of my subconscious
Where there are no edges to mine

But you are my saaanity!
And my love for what it's worth
You are my places been, my space within
My favorite sin
My down to earth

<u>Sonnet I</u>

Tell me, what thoughts have I of your bright smile?
Thinking in moon lit rooms and star filled skies
'Twas my empty arms that bitters my bile
For visions of you are with day-dreamed eyes
'Twas passionate pains on my heart that tugs
Its jealousy holding my precious gift
'Twas vibrant arms on my pillow that hugs
My love, where art thou and who art thou with?
So I watch as my dreams fly with the birds
For your residence removes from my fate
Thoughts are ineffable for Webster's words
But I know they lay between love and hate
I will surprise her, be a survivor
Yet such short-term love I can't decipher

Sonnet II

What makes your beauty shine close to my eyes?
And makes thou worthy of my poem's pen?
Two years we played faith on misery's' lies
And painted excuses for mortal men
Beauty shines before the due date of love
So let your passion be within my reach
But times I extended for you above
There were new lessons for heaven to teach
But you shall remain that treasure of mine
Completely mummified if thou must die
Resurrected in 400 years time
Calmly, hoping you hear my humble cry
Burping a nation, through maternity
Living our lives for eternity

Sonnet III

Ha! She had the nerve to call my crazy
Ha! She says I fall in love to quickly
But the words that she spat did not phase me
I knew that she wanted to be with me
For those endless stares just swallowed me whole
Her every thought pattern gave me vision
I read within crevices of her soul
And she gave me rights for such incision
Why don't you bathe me in your warm embrace?
And take my doubt out of its misery
Show me reflections of your youthful face
Your soul will leave some room for mystery
And I will place my hand up on my brow
Knowing you as queen, on my knees I bow

Unorthodox Sonnet

Can loving eyes see?
Well I must contest no!
For she played me off key
And I swear I didn't know
I gave her strokes of passion
And I couldn't understand
Why in my sheets of satin
She was with another man
What trickery is this?
I blame it upon the evil
Such anger clenched my fists
And my heart I labeled feeble
She asked to be friends- what to say? What to do?
I leaned over and calmly said @#%$ you!

Struggle...

No Longer

I traveled across seas to be hurtled upon this land
A land that left me amazed
There were different gods praised
And I just couldn't understand
Who had the nerve to disrupt me?
Who had the gumption?
Why did you bring me here and what is my function?
I left my life to be shifted at new momentum
And as I felt the whip on my back
I tasted the serpent's venom
Is this my destiny?
This isn't my place!
I am a man of royalty, if my history was traced
Back when the skies were blue
We use to carve on bamboo
And what was really true was the smile on my face
Where my people sang in sync
New mathematics we would think
And every time I blink
There was an herb I would taste
But you have me here in fear
Where my thoughts aren't clear
Herbs are rare
And due to your consumption
Natural resources disappear
Why do you have me in such a manner?
You were such an unlawful planner

Took my blood, land and color
Replaced by your banner
So I tended to your abode
In hopes that my anger never showed
Soon stories would be told
Of my four hundred year old road
And through my children
I would live the life I have to live
In hopes that their dreams and aspirations
Would be the life they want to live
And no longer will we live in misery
I will teach them about there history
Teach them how life should be
I will open up their eyes so that they can see
That we can no longer be "I" we have to be "WE"
And do you know what we will be?
Do you know what we will be?
We will be
FREE!
FREE!
No longer will things be the same
No longer will I bear the blame
No longer will my land you claim
No longer will I be in shame
No longer will you leave a stain
No longer will I pick your grain
No longer!
No longer!
No longer!
No longer!

As time goes on and my children are born
Our hearts will grow stronger
And I will walk
That four hundred years of miles in length
Just to rebuild my strength
So I could no longer be 3/5ths or even 6/10ths
No longer shall we live in struggle
No longer shall we live in pain
No longer will you change my name
No longer will we live in chains
No longer!

Tarbaby

I am a tarbaby, denounced by my race
A race full of blacks, but I the blacker face
What makes you so envious?
That your jealousy roars?
Is this because the sun favors me more?
Hmm...

My Home In Italy

It reminds me of my home in Italy
That is if I ever was there
Way past the pond, past the trees
I see
I see civilization
I see mountains almost invisible to sight
What is civilization?
But one little home
Like my home in Italy
That is if I ever was there
For all I see is green
Be it the trees
Be it the grass
Or be it my envy
For I could only dream of such a beautiful place
A path that splits the trees
A pond that splits the trees
And trees that split the path from the pond
It is beautiful
Just like my home in Italy
That is if I ever was there

Brooklyn (you lied to me)

Oh Brooklyn, oh Brooklyn
What have I to lose?
From corruption to destruction
What have I to choose?
Liquor stores on every corner
Human beings wrapped in blues
And everyday I hear them calling
Your name on the news
Oh Brooklyn, oh Brooklyn
It is me you have misled
My children raped and sodomized
And others shot in the head
Brooklyn is peaceful
I heard it once said
It seems our reason for living
Prefers to be dead
You lied to me Brooklyn
It seems things are getting worse
You've held guns and smoked pipes
And I saw you snatch that woman's purse
Instead of killing and stealing
Why can't we love?
Why can't we barter?
Why choose to be a part of such foolish martyr?
I have been bombarded
Disregarded
And in instances attacked

I have been neglected
Disrespected
And expected to adapt
In order to survive I must have a nine-to-five
Can't you tell, I am living in a hell
So how can I stay alive?
Miss Liberty, I never met her
For you choose to keep me fettered
You lied to me Brooklyn
I thought things were getting better

Peace Doesn't Live Here Anymore

Let me tell you what happened to peace
He moved away from here
Because he couldn't stand the west and east
I searched for peace once, but I couldn't find him
And when the gunshots went off around my way never mind him
Peace always came back every now and then friend
But no one seems to know when, when was when
And about that time
When brothers showed up in coffins
Peace didn't really seem to come that often
Where was he in those times of need?
He always had the cure when people had envied
Who knew he had enemies?
That always offended him
Such as greed and namely racism
Peace against war, peace should win by a landslide
But some of peace friends always go to the bad side
When brothers have shootouts, they don't really care
I can see why peace moved away from here
But you see I am not worrying he will soon come up
When some of peace friends they tend to sum up
But if you come in my neighborhood
Knocking on my door
Asking for peace...he doesn't live here anymore

Dem Poets

Sing-"Dem poets dem poets dem poets
Wanna rule my destiny"
It is written, in black and white
That they are as separate as day from night
You see, I want you to look to your left
And I want you to look to your right
Have you realized?
That there are evil poets among us?
I said there are evil poets among us
Dem poets that show many different faces
In many different places
Prone to be two toned in many different cases
Dem judge and jury poets that do not have a clue
You are judging him, you are judging me
But who the hell is judging you?
Dem poets that talk so much about you
It makes you wonder, you start to figure
In front my face you call me brother
Behind my back you call me nigger
I have no time for your jargons
No time for your ways
I block my ears from your pardons
And shade my eyes from your rays
There are evil poets among us
And I can count them one by one
Dem poets that claim to be non-violent
Yet still hides behind their gun

Telling me to bow to no one
But their souls have ashy knees
They wore slavery bells and swam the Atlantic
Now Sprint from AT&T
Dem prestigious pretentious preaching pastor poets
That claim to be men of the cloth
In his words of abundance I see no substance
All I taste is broth
Telling me to control my dome
When you can't control your booze
Another poet said, "save the animals"
And she is wearing leather shoes
If I followed you I would be in the pits
You've got me throwing fits
My people learn to use your wits
And forget about those hypocrites
We must choose a better way
A clearer path, a different route
There are evil poets among us
If you see them, pick them out
Dem poets that are afraid to dream
The impossible dream
So they call it unimaginable
Dem poets that say revolution one hundred times
Because they know its fashionable
That poet that's labeled odd
So to find himself he searches
Now he calls himself god
But cries sanctuary in churches
Dem ebonics-hooked-on-phonics poets

That claim to know many languages
Dem poets that say they are vegetarians
And eating ham sandwiches
They talk their talk; they walk their walk
But their heart is filled with gelatin
Enough pork to fill New York
And they call it Holistic Medicine
You see I am not a poet
I am the voice of America's youth
Some people label me a poet
But I just speak the truth
And the truth is
To follow dem would be the pits
You have got me throwing fits
My people learn to use your wits
And forget about those hypocrites
There are evil poets among us
But they shall never see the best in me
Sing--"Dem poets, dem poets, dem poets
Want to rule my destiny"

So Many...So little (song)

So many religions
And so little time
So many gods
And so little minds
So many facts
And so little proof
So many bibles
And so little truth
Where am I to go?
And who shall I follow?
The answers I don't know
What truth shall I swallow?

Feel My Frustration!

I, the son of a man who stands firm in his actions,
decisions, ways and in the path he follows. I am not a
chemist or a biologist nor have I studied any science of the
sciences, so I depart from his path and follow my own.
Which such variety, how is one to know which is wrong,
which is right, which is bad which is good? I am a man of
solitude mind, a prisoner when not a prisoner, alone when
not alone. I think of all the rage inside, which only I know
of, for I lie with my external face.
Who else feels like I feel?
Who else feels the same anger?
When all that are against you are your superiors
Some envy your youth, or fear your complexion
They know nothing of you, know not of your intellect
But they judge you by their ignorance
Defined as experience and intelligence
Do you feel my frustration?

Monkey

And so they labeled me a monkey
Or shall I say us
They hanged us from trees
While our women they lust
And so they called me tarbaby
A nigga for short
Tried to rob us of our land
And so the monkey fought
Later on down the line as you turn the pages
The monkey spent his bananas to own his own cages
Go head and raise you white fist
But like you, the monkey is now labeled a capitalist

What Is Life?

I try to conjure thoughts in my head
To define what is life
Is it a house with a picket fence?
Two children and a wife?
And a dog, a dog that barks?
Having picnics in parks?
Then death provides a stairway to heaven
Serenaded by harps
What is life?
Is it a concept developed by man?
Put in statements like life is a struggle?
Or I hold your life in my hands?
Or is life some sort of quiz, an examination or a test?
And the only way of passing is by cheating death?
What is life?
Is it watching a loved one
Getting gunned down in cold blood?
Would you see life as a dud?
Or rebuild faith from the mud?
You see struggle can be a sickness
But to death you seek immunity
Education becomes the cure
Then life becomes opportunity
What is life?
But fables in newspapers that are frequently heard
But don't say life at dinner tables
Because it's a four letter word

Or is life some sort of journey?
An expedition or a quest?
That's tampered with by risk?
And measured by success?
An executive on Wall Street
Realizes he cannot hack it
A youth prefers to lose his life
Instead of his leather jacket
What is life?
Is life witnessing a loved one's very last breath?
Then meeting him later on in life?
But wait!
Isn't that death?
Oh from the powers that be
Too blinding for the eyes that can see
If this is what is life
Don't restrain it
Explain it to me
What is life to a father that has lost his son?
What is life to a mother that protects her young?
What was life to the corpse of a famous designer?
What is life to the hearts and souls of our minor?
If you know someone who is educated, fought through a
struggle or raised children
I beg you to thank the Lord
For the blessings he has given
So if they ask you what is life
You say life is worth living
That is life

Motivation...

I Can Move Mountains

Inspired by Dr. F. E Roy Jeffries

Seeds were implanted in me
Down under the soil of Christianity
Still centered in the mind are animalistic views
I've been amused by those fools who try to control
Why only heritage has my soul
Academically designed to incline
Defined as a problem
But it's all in the mind
Sing-"Sometimes I feel like a motherless child"
The earth gave birth now has rotted
Plans of a better nation we have plotted
But gluttons push the wrong buttons
Causing explosions, mass erosions
On the earth's surface
They have the nerve to get nervous
How dare you say that all men are created equal
When poverty and welfare regulate my people
My people
My people it's time to move mountains
We have nothing to lose
We just stand on the highest plain
And yell "Yo mountain **MOOVE**"
Sing-"But brothers hold grudges "
Because the mountain never budges
And idleness comes large
And motivation is mentally discharged

Sing-"Can somebody tell me how to move a mountain?
My people run deep like water
Flowing from an endless fountain
Don't you understand that we have nothing to lose?
We just stand on the highest plain and yell
Yo mountain, **MOOOVE**!
But leaders don't show faces"
Afraid to take their places in the populace
How can you be so bold?
To give benefits to the old
When I have been treated cold
Before and after I was four hundred years old
And sexism does exist
But can I make a list
Of all my black sisters
That had to raise their black fists
My people have been criticized, mutilated, brutalized
How can you speak of sexism and ageism?
When racism is institutionalized
My people its time to move mountains
Just nudge them out your path
All aims, objectives and goals
Shall soon be in your grasp
Just follow me, I will lead the way
Who am I you might say
Who Am I? Who Am I?
I push hills aside and tall landscapes I devour
I think critically, analytically
Plus politically I have power
I can pull clouds out the sky

I can move mountains by the bulk
I swallowed Mount Fuji in one gulp
Beat Mt. Kenya to a pulp
I grounded the Rockies till it tasted like syrup
Leaped over the Appalachians
Towards my travels into Europe
Mercy, mercy even as we speak
You know they are crying mercy
Upon Communism Peak
Even when I sneeze, the cool breeze across seas
Can bring the Alps to my knees
And still stop off in Vienna
To taste the chocolate and cheese
There is no peace in Greece for the gods are at a halt
I capsized Mt. Olympus
And wrestled Zeus for his lighting bolt
My people cried, "Victory, Victory"
But I have more in store
For I go back to the United States
And chisel my face in Mt. Rushmore
And as I leave South Dakota
I want all my people to follow
For I travel to the Mother Land
To beat drums on Kilamonjaro
I passed by the pyramids but I left them alone
They had no geometrical equations
Plus it said black ,"Victory, Victory"
I see no victory today
For Mount Everest still stands to be my finest prey
And so I climb Mr. Everest and I look him eye to eye

And said no longer would your head remain above the
clouds in the sky
I came down and told my people
Mount Everest must fall
One half in Tibet, the other half in Nepal
My people just laughed and others seemed uncertain
And yet in times of struggle and action
They questioned my person
I said, "Maybe they don't know who I am"
Who Am I?
And what I can do
Who am I?
And what I can do?
I can gargle bodies of water by the gallons and cases
Spit them in desert spaces to form an oasis
I can make the leaning Tower of Pisa
Stand firm and tall
Make the Statue of Liberty have a very bad fall
Yes I am black and the black man's epitome
I can kick Sicily off the boot of Italy
All mountains shall shake
From the power that I create
People in other countries
Would swear it was an earthquake
So please Mr. Everest, let me spare you today
I said Mountain move out of my way!

If I Were To Dream

If I were to dream, then let me dream you a tale
Traveling the seven sees with treasures to unveil
I am a ship's captain upon oceans I sail
Conquering all oppressors and successors
Dare not do I fail
If I were to dream, then let me dream up a chance
To shatter glass ceilings make my people advance
Why I am a king, I hold life in my hands
I have power in my crown... and wealth in my pants
If I were to dream let me travel the endless skies
Passing from cloud to cloud
Every time I blink my eyes
Why I am a pilot, why do you look so surprised?
I have knowledge of aviation
Can cause objects to rise
RISE! RISE! RISE!
Sing-"I have dreams to remember"
And if I were to share my dreams with you
How can I find the words?
To tell my people if they try
They can fly like the birds
You may say how can this be
I close my eyes so I can see
Or is it just my imagination running away with me
I have achieved because of will
Some say because of luck
I could make oceans stand still and volcanoes erupt

I dream past to present
Gave my people mind and presence
Taught my children all their lessons
Brought them back to their essence
You have to control your thoughts
That are seen and unseen
My people, my people we have to learn how to dream
When failure wanted me, nightmares haunted me
I learned how to dream undauntedly
From all that I feel it's so hard to reveal
How fairytales and novels
Can all of a sudden become real
I visited Anne of Green Gables
Been through Aesop's Fables
I fought with King Arthur and sat at round tables
Open your mind, as thoughts seem to unravel
For now I'm intertwined within Gulliver's travels
Curiosity, gives thought patterns velocity
As I possibly travel on another Odyssey
I entered John Steinbeck's world
Where I heard of The Pearl
But I couldn't tell the difference
Between Men and Mice
Sailed with Robinson Crusoe off Tobago
And played Beloved Jazz
In a Toni Morrison's Paradise
Paradise?
Paradise is Powerful Paragraphs
Potential Pressure Paralyzes
Prose, Poetry and Puns, Promotes Pulitzer Prizes

Pad and Pencil in my Palms
Protect a Princess in a Palace
Stop and drink a spot of tea
In wonderland with Alice
I ate with kings, queens, lords
Dukes, duchesses and an earl
I told an artist formerly known as Prince
To hold his Diamonds and Pearls
Somebody called me Tarbaby
But that name doesn't suit me
I transformed into a horse
And they labeled me Black Beauty
Found divine justice in Nemesis
I flew off the wings of Pegasus
Cured all the white man's fetishes
On black man premises
I horrified hypocrisies
Downsized democracies
Flipped all philosophies installed by Socrates
I pulled the throttle on Aristotle
Had time to invent the wheel
Threw a bottle at Adonis the model
While holding Achilles by the heel
I never dreamed of the impossible dream
For I dream as far as the stars
Close my eyes with one thought I can leap unto mars
I wanted to go to Venus
But that is the land of the brave
They said the majority was women
And all men were enslaved

Since there is too little room I will have to harpoon
Onto Jupiter and cocoon around its sixteen moons
I rode the rings of Saturn
And swung by the Big Dipper
And came right back in time
To give Cinderella her slipper
And meet all adoring fans
I'm surfing seas over sinking sands
Why I could walk on water
Holding my Creator's hands
Can this all be true or will you call this luck?
Can all my dreams come true?
And will I ever wake up?
I said how could this be?
That when I close my eyes I see
I see my people who are mentally free
I see doctors and lawyers on my family tree
I see my brothers not in the army
But being all that they can be
Evading birds and circling around clouds
Is it greatness that I see?
Or is it just my imagination running away with me?

Inspiration

Oh lord no trouble can enter in me
Because I run my life so practically
I dare not wonder what road I should go
Cause father you promised me tomorrow
For I am inspiration
Some analyze my life
Just call me inspiration
No compromise
No sacrifice
I hold my own
While some hold trust in me
Just call on my emotions and I will be
Your inspiration
I climb the Rockies
Back souls I bring
They came so quietly
But now they sing
I said don't worry
Just hear my voice
And I will give you reason
To rejoice
Just call me inspiration

62

I am

I am
That identifiable brother
That can't find his way home
That was afraid of the dark and scared to be alone
I couldn't enunciate my R's
I swung on monkey bars
I day dreamed about the stars
And owning property on Mars
I am
A member of that race that created his own slang
Some say I do my thing, but "I be doin my thang"
Some call me top notch
Cause I play Skelly and Hopscotch
And I just discovered manhood by holding my crouch
I am
The first one to start a rumor
That your fetus has a tumor
I am that #1 consumer
To wear Adidas and suede Pumas
Check my sneakers yo!
Check my sneakers!
I am that one that stood on the corner
Drinking for the hell of it
Teasing teens cause they're virgins
But since birth I've been celibate
I use to Pop and do the Wop
And the invention of break dancing

Flat-chested girls I us to be romancing
Sing-"Cool no sweat I will go get your soda pop
The candy establishment is just around the block"
And as I drunk my Forty
I leaned to the side to look Sporty
And everybody I knew was named
Yo Shorty! Yo Shorty!
Wipe my sneakers Yo!
You stepped on my sneakers!
But from whom the bell tolls
Lay no eyes upon my grave
God have mercy on my soul
Let my spirit please be saved
At a glance I have advanced evolving from the slave
But is this the road that my ancestors paved?
Who am I?
One man calls me life another man calls me breath
One man calls me height
Another man calls me depth
You see God made man and man made clone
Man calls me god, but they say it means unknown
And you know me!
I create whirlwinds at a whim
And tear egos off their limbs
Still have time to buss a rhyme
And sing Christians hymns
I am talking old Negro spirituals
That makes the cotton picker say, *"Drop it!"*
I put the soul into hums and beat drums on a bucket
I held conferences with the stars

And gave them all assignments
I can push Pluto next to mars
And cause a new solar alignment
I took justice for a ride
Through ancient times I survived
When Moses parted the Red Sea...
I was on the other side
And you want to know who I am?
I gave Columbus a tour for he didn't have a clue
I taught the art of war to a man named Sun Tzu
The Romans tried to capture me
I told them to bear arms
And I perplexed them permanently
By pushing pyramids out my palms
King Tut couldn't handle this
And here is something for the funnies
I wrapped Pharaohs into bandages
And had them crying for their mummies
They told me time was running out when the Millennium
lingered in the mist
But I wrap time around my little finger
While I watch it wrap around your wrist
Mankind called me justice, but mankind couldn't tell
Sing-"That justice is just a war between heaven and hell"
Upon my arrival they called me a disciple
I drunk from King James Cup
And spat words from the bible
I objected to false laws
And traveled through hatreds jaws
Holy wars was my rage in the age of the Moors

Since creation I concoct equations for fun
All persuasions said
How amazing is that raisin in the sun
So to ask me who I am you must believe in fiction
To imagine what can't be fathomed is my addiction
They pinned me from arm to arm
And planned my crucifixion
But I am the bearer of eternal life
They can cause me no affliction
Traveling through time and space with grace
Beyond man's jurisdiction
With the letters A-N-K-H
On my throat as an inscription
So if anyone comes through that door
And asks for my description
Tell them I am a dark-skinned, black king
That walks like an Egyptian
Talks like an Egyptian, roars like a lion
Oh blessed, animal tested and manifested in Zion
Climbing up justice ladder
When I come evil scatters
I am...what I am!
And that's all that matters.

Pass Me The Ball

A sensation in the nation
A white mans fascination
"Defense!"
A man shouts
At a black man's ticket out
Not academics, but a sport
Found in my back yard
In the streets of New York
We all dreamt of being a point guard
Ten seconds on the clock
I will make the shot
I will be the hero
I made that shot with eyes closed
Twenty degrees below zero
Brother don't come cause I won't hesitate my handle
You come left, I will go right
As I pursue to break your ankles
There is a new star in town haven't you heard
I am Magic Johnson, Isaiah Thomas
Air Jordan, Larry Bird
I dribble balls behind my back
I will make a pass that would make you figure
I can shoot your eyes out
As if my hand was a trigger
Some score by skills, others score by luck
But I elevate to the whole and yell
Everybody get up!

Pass Me the Ball!

The Lion Undaunted

I dodged time and gauged prosperity
Cleverly entered in a disguised realm
Closed the doors on inhumanity
And placed compassion at the helm
How long shall I live in discontentment?
Before I reach the pinnacle of success
In the eyes of others I see resentment
For I seem different from the rest
They know nothing of my character
Know nothing for what I strive
But survival dwells in my stamina
Realize, for I am alive!
Surviving from what is cowering me, souring me
The powers that be devouring me
As unrevealed dynasties begin to unfold
My only plan is to be in allegiance with my soul
So hide within crevices, tell your false tales
Know that my justice is not weighed upon your scales
Oh no emotion in my heart
Can divulge such unearthly feelings
It tears me apart dealing with these human beings
Giving me two pennies
Looking at me in scorn
Telling me breathe the breath of many
Yet my shoes remain unworn
I am classified inferior
So they labeled me a pawn

Cause I don't fit their criteria
Handing me the crown of thorns
But I still remain the lion undaunted
Walking the paths where I am not wanted
Name calling fate and holding destiny by the throat
Shining heavens pearly gates
Upon life's waters I stay afloat
I will not drown and give you the satisfaction
Half of me want down
But you will never see that fraction
No longer will you fool me for such cruelty is brutal
Silence is for the choice-less
To remain voiceless is futile
I am that spoken vessel
And I urge you all to listen
With struggle we must wrestle
Until he breaks into submission
Choke him - yoke him
Hold him in position
And do not release him
Till he asks for my permission
I am the lion undaunted
They wonder how through trouble times I can soar
Mere mortals shall bow from the sound of my roar
I grazed the likes of envy and hatred I had fooled
For the pain they have inflicted
I challenge the wicked to a duel
No need for petty trinkets
Strength and bravery be my wealth
I am looking evil in his eyes and seeing fear, himself

I am still dodging time and holding down the fort
Playing life like a board game
And survival like a sport
I am Iron, like a Lion still standing strong
Plucking the strings of Justice creating my own song

How Do We Know?

I formed a shield around my existence
In the class of 9th grade
I felt like Charlie brown
As my teacher's voice began to fade
Closing my eyes by no surprise
To all those that intruded
Because I was distant from the rest
And always felt excluded
You see
I was different
While others talked their talk I sang my song
I put semi-colons, commas and question marks where they
didn't belong
While others proclaimed things to be fact
The majority accepted it to be so
I was the one to stand back
And say, "how do we know?"
Must I be degraded for being a right brain thinker?
Oh how the teacher hated
That with theory I would tinker
You see it started when he spoke about man
And woman deriving from man
And how they are all human
And with this man ending
You can closely relate and understand
But I thought

Surely he must jest about the mothers of our nation
How do we know that the word Man
Constitutes a Woman's derivation?
I said "Professor can I ask you a question?"
He said, "go head shoot."
I said, "If a grape is a fruit
Then what in the world is a grapefruit?"
He looked astonished
And his thoughts were in disarray
So to buy time to answer my question
He said, "What did you say?"
I said, "If a grape is a fruit
Then what the hell is a grapefruit?
You see one is much smaller
And they don't have the same shape
A grapefruit looks like an orange
And most certainly cannot derive from the grape
So if a grape is a fruit then what the hell is a ----"
"Mr. Kayo!
This is a forty-five minute session
Do not interrupt me with such foolish questions"
I heard the echoes of his words
As my classmates laughed
Shriveling my sense of dignity
Leaving me feeling daft
But on my side was Drew, Einstein
Carver, Bell, Socrates and Plato
And we all belted at once "If you didn't know the answer to
the question
All you had to do was say so!"

And of course he felt disrespected and he said
"I beg ya pardon"
Called me ignorant, stubborn and harden
And put me in the corner like Kindergarten
After all that humiliation
I pledged never to do it again
But how could you mute something
That comes from within
So one day he spoke about space and the planets
And good old mother earth
And continued by assuming
We were alone in this great universe
I wanted to erupt in my seat
For it seems the teacher has been had
"Em, Em Mr. Kayo
Is there something that you can add?"
I was trapped in a room filled with deadly stares
But I sucked in all my fears
And looked at all my peers
And said...
I said, "How do we know there is no life on Mars?"
My classmates' eyes opened up wide
And witnessed I was beyond adolescence
And the professor looked at me in angst
Because of my presence
How do we know there is no life on Mars?
Scientists say this to be a fact
But these are the same people
Who told me the world was flat
And historians wrote of their recoveries

But these are the same people
That told me of false discoveries
He showed me a picture in a book
And professed my theory to be a flop
But teacher, that was kerned and cropped
On QuarkXpress and PhotoShop
And a story was concoct for anyone that harasses
And they published it in millions of books
Just to calm the masses
Don't get me wrong, I am not headstrong
I am not saying it isn't so
But due to deception and misconception
The question is, "How do we know?"
To say that we are alone can be a complete fallacy
How do we know we are alone in this single galaxy?
I mean the nerve of you
You speak as if you've lived amongst the stars
How do we really know there is no life on Mars?
You see I traveled the universe
From the head of my bed
And watched Charles Drew
Draw blood from the earth and made Mars red
Since the birth of earth
We were breaking down walls
But on Neptune, Alexander Graham Bell
Is making outer global calls
They thought there was no life on Venus
But know one really knows this
But the Venusians heard a space shuttle sound
And went underground

With Harriet Tubman and Moses
And on Uranus, if you can
Without blinking man
Look beyond you will see Rodin
Sitting like the thinking man
There are many faces and many races
Beyond technology's wings
And I saw Flo Jo and Jesse Owens
Running around Saturn's rings
Running to the rhythm of time
But I think I forgot to mention
By design Einstein defined time as a dimension
I know there is life on Jupiter
I know my eyes do not fail
There I saw George Washington Carver
With peanuts for sale
There, Shakespeare wrote sonnets
And Beethoven had an epiphany
Played the Congo on the Bongo
And called it a symphony
And when I said there were nine planets
They all looked at me and laughed
I said, "I read them in my text book
Count them, you do the math"
Besides this book cost me an arm and a leg
It's the top of the line
Check out this fine design, this spine of mine
First published in 1969
Shakespeare said, "don't mean to offend my lord
But my lord you must be ill

Can't you see that book is written
With some technological quill?"
I said, "What trickery is this?
Must you play me for some buffoon?"
I knew there were nine planets
Since man landed on the moon
So if there are not nine planets
Then how do you know?
That's when they pointed at the tenth planet
It was right behind Pluto
So don't tell me there is no life on Mars
And even worse, this universe
I am a child my mind runs wild
Don't feed me info that was rehearsed
Let me question the unquestionable
Do not stifle what I say
Because this is what's limiting my children today
How do you know teacher?
How do you know?

Page Turner

She was a page-turner
But her pages were not simple to the naked eye
Her pages came in facial expressions
And internal misery
Counseling sessions
And past time paintings of mystery
So I tried to read her book from cover to cover
Read passages of her abusive mother
Poetic verses of her innate brother
And tore out pages of her thoughtless lover
So I-- I
I was intrigued
Intrigued at her need to repel
Repel from outside interference
Who only saw her external appearance
But to read her book you had to have clearance
So I-- I
I continued
And read on as if the pages were in my own hand
Learned of many obstacles that were invisible to man
The oxygen I gave her
I would save her if I can
But she wanted no favors
No, that wasn't in her plan
She begged for no mercy
No helping hand, no kindly deed
She wanted me to stay thirsty

To just sit there and read
So I--I
I drank the pain
In the echoes of her words
Agony whispered her name
Silencing songs of the birds
She could be filled with animosity
Mad at the world, a hater
But that she couldn't possibly be
Because that wasn't in her nature
She absorbed every strike with resistance
Took every blow on the chin
Negated struggle with persistence
As she searched for the power within
Her soul became iron
Her heart was like steel
She called unto Zion
For a life more surreal
I--I
Ideal even
But Idealism only happens in the mind
But if she searched deep enough
She would be able to find
That an inferior nature can no longer be defined
Only designed
But now what does she have left?
Down to a very last breath
Life took away her strength
And now what's left is death
I-I

I have nothing left of this dear friend
Tears blurred the ink of her life's pen
To dismiss her life I couldn't pretend
I'll read her book till its end

So I--I--I
I will tell her story!
I will tell her story to motivate the young
Carving it on the trees where our ancestors hung
I will tell it in Spoken Word forums and books
Capturing the essence
In fancy punch lines and hooks
I will tell it to the students of the fondling professor
In hotels and motels where bibles lay on the dresser
In abusive relationships
Where women make no decisions
In African Villages
Where women go through circumcision
To the worn down woman forever lying on her back
To the lady in the corner taking heroin and crack
To the Tomboys
Who are considered troublemakers
And rabble-rousers
To the daughter who can't prevail
Over jail and group houses
To the welfare mother
Who is watching her life plummet
To the out of wedlock woman
Who has a swollen stomach
To the lost and unaware child

That can't find her roots under the ground
To the woman that calls herself queen
But can't find her crown
In every beauty salon in every ghetto, in every city
To every youth that thinks she's so damn un-pretty
I will tell it to the mother in college
Who wishes to advance
To the woman who had an abortion
And wants a second chance
To the bright young child who wishes to excel
I will tell her story!
And I will tell it well.